Enoch Black

Incubus Tales

Enoch Black

Incubus Tales

A Collection of Poems on Sexual Trauma,
Sexventures, and Mindful Sex

By Enoch Black

Curious Corvid Publishing

Ohio

Incubus Tales: A Collection of Poems on Sexual Trauma, Sexventures, and Mindful Sex by Enoch Black

Published by Curious Corvid Publishing, LLC.

Cover design by Ravven White

Printed in the United States of America

Cataloging-in-Publication Data is on file with the Library of Congress.
ISBN: 978-1-7376916-1-7
ISBN (ebook): 978-1-7376916-2-4
www.curiouscorvidpublishing.com

Introduction

I grew up in two worlds that at first glimpse do not appear to be compatible, and perhaps to some degree they are not; and yet, both played integral parts in the story of my childhood abuse and trauma. Please don't misunderstand me. It is not my intention to call out any one person or societal structure. All structures are capable of being used for abuse from the microcosm that is the mind to the largest governments in the world. Just because these entities are capable of abuse or even when they do perpetrate it, that does not necessarily mean that they are inherently abusive by nature. No, we all make choices within those structures, within the matrices in which we live. Thus, I faced abuse on two fronts and they kept me in a place I did not flourish.

I have very vivid memories of sexuality playing a part in my life. I can still remember the first time I experienced an erection as a child. I remember the first time ejaculation occurred from masturbation. They were pivotal moments in my life, not because of what they were, but rather because of how those in my life responded to them. I was systematically shamed for them, both at a familiar and religious level. Please don't think I am looking for pity or sympathy. I don't want it. No, I am grateful for those experiences because they have granted me the opportunity to be there for others in a healthy, healing manner that I was not given. I am also not suggesting that it was better that I was sexually shamed. It wasn't. It still isn't. It would have been better that I never lived such things, but I am grateful for them nonetheless because I have allowed them to empower me instead of to enthrall me as their slave. I hope this collection of poetry might be able to provide opportunity to at least one person with a little bit of that same empowerment. May sexual healing be your personal power.

Poet's Note

The poetry you are about to read is based, at least loosely, on my life. It's a collection of my sexual trauma, sexual misadventures and adventures, and sexual healing. It also includes some mindful erotic and sensual poetry at the end. The events behind these poetic stories are not necessarily chronologically provided here according to the chapter. Healing is never as sequential as most of us would hope it to be. We often follow the old adage of taking two proverbial steps forward and one back. That has and does certainly describe my own life. Nevertheless, I do want to share some insights into the five chapters and their themes. I have chosen to use words that all begin with the letter *M* for each chapter simply because I enjoyed the idea. *Murder* is primarily about sexual trauma I have experienced in my life. *Misadventures* concerns some of my sexual mishaps along the path of healing. I wish I could say that I have never hurt another human being within the realm of a romantic relationship, but the truth is that I have. No doubt, I will again. Love and lust are beautiful monsters. *Miracles* tells stories of sexual healing in my life. *Mythologies* is the naughtiness of the chapters as it may or may not recount some of my own real life sexual adventures. Finally, *Mindfulness* provides some poems about mindful sexual attitudes and acts. Ultimately, this collection is as much for my own healing as it is an attempt on my part to bring sex positivity and healing to others. Sexuality is a major part of who and what we are as human beings. We wield it as a weapon, both sword and shield. It can also be healing…and just fucking fun! Thank you, dear reader, for joining me for a small moment. I hope it brings you laughter, light, love, and even a little bit of lust. Embrace your incubus or succubus. Let them tell their stories. After all, their stories are your stories. Much love to you all.

Table of Contents aka The Devil's in the Details...

Chapter One – Murder

Chapter Two – Misadventures

Chapter Five – Mindfulness

Chapter 1 – Murder

my killing endures

murder is not always death

my body lives on

Abuse Begins With No End

Abuse begins with no end,

Always cycling through another generation, more
souls to rend.

My mother's story was no different but still her
own,

One of abuse and trauma like a rope necklace
carrying a giant stone.

It dragged her to the deepest pits,

The darkest Sheol that steals both humor and wits.

She lived there for so long,

When she finally escaped she had no idea what was
right and what was wrong.

Abuse and conflict had become her home,

A prison from which she would never roam.

She carried it with her in body and mind,

Never aware she could not accept healthy love to which she was blind.

Fear of Conflict

I remember my dad's stories of my grandfather
punching him in the face.

My dad couldn't remember why, but he still felt
deeply the disgrace.

He loved his father and forgave him all his abuse,

But he carried that burden like some demonic muse.

I never understood this need to forgive

Until I realized he couldn't live with anything
combative.

So, he stood on the sidelines while we, his children,
endured another round of abuse,

A collective sledgehammer, a metaphorical noose.

My dad was a good man,

But his inability to act was the door through which
the abuse began.

Letting Go and Moving On

There were many horrors in my childhood,

Not only sexual but also violent, burning me up like so much firewood.

Memories flood my mind's gate,

My mom chasing me with a knife as my fate.

My dad pinning me to a wall,

Taking away my breath till finally he allows me to fall.

Years later they beg and plead to be a part of my life,

But I know now all that would bring is strife.

Pet Projects

Some stories do not have a happily ever after.

Some books don't have another chapter.

Instead, they are more like a record put on repeat.

They always have the same rhythm, the same old beat.

A brother molested by a neighbor,

As he got older he wielded these wounds like a saber.

It wasn't long before he attempted the same,

But our mother said he was not to blame.

He had been abused and couldn't help it.

He couldn't climb out of that pit.

My anger over the years though was at a slow boil.

Our family was nothing but rotten soil.

First, he attempted it with a small child,

But everyone forgave him and there was no exile.

Then he completed the act with our sister,

But my mother insisted it was his trauma, that ripe blister.

She sought to save him, he was her pet project,

The rest of us remained neglected no matter how wrecked.

Perhaps it's easier to gaze into mirrors and see someone with a similar reflection in order to want to love them.

Through the Looking Glass

I still remember the first day I heard someone say,
"Hey, your brother's gay."

I thought to myself, No way. We are Christian and
that's the way we will stay.

I was young and ignorant and didn't understand.

Besides, it wasn't like my own sexual self-control
had gone as planned.

Anyway, this classmate tells me a kid is picking on
my brother.

This is my flesh and blood, another child of my
mother.

My reaction is to see red

Wanting nothing more than to make this bully dead.

I tell my buddy to show me who this is.

We walk down another hall and find him at his
locker where I say, "Hey, pop quiz."

"Do you know who I am?"

"You're so and so's brother, but I don't give a damn."

That's when I slam him against his locker

And explain I'm now his personal stalker.

If he ever teases or touches my brother again,

I'm going to do all that I can,

To make his life miserable

And I promise it will be considerable.

He looks at me with fear in his eyes

And agrees quickly which is wise.

What I did was a horrible thing,

Acting like some wannabe violent king.

Still, it makes me wonder.

I stood up for my brother, but myself I would rip
asunder.

It didn't matter to me if my brother was gay or not,

But my lack of self-control was a horrible blot.

It was stain on me, my lack of faith to overcome.

It threatened and beat me like I might have that kid,
not stopping till I was nothing but numb.

Confessions

Living half truths and hiding half lies.

These were my nightmarish lullabies.

I was caught in a twilight world,

One filled with a violent wind that whipped and
whirled.

Any day where I masturbated at all,

I felt like I had given in completely to Adam's Fall.

I still read my journal entries from those days,

Where I walked around numb and half in a daze.

The guilt would eat at me like some giant worm,

Like I was pregnant with evil and had come to term.

I would birth orally to my wife and bishop all that I
had done…

More tears would follow that made me want to run.

That was the cycle of my life for years,

Masturbation, Confession, and Community Tears.

Therapies

I went through a plethora of therapists throughout
the years,

So many meetings filled with anger, defensiveness,
and tears.

Most of them belonged to the same religion,

I thought it would help me make the right decision.

Looking back now, I realize I was the round peg,

Trying to fit a mismatched hole was nothing short
of a powder keg.

The last therapist that I had looked me in the face

And told me I was too smart for my own good and
thus undeserving of grace.

He said I would forever find loopholes to God's
commands   ·

And because of that I was standing on a foundation
made of sand.

I would continue to sink under the surface till I
wanted to repent,

His words left me broken and spent.

That One Evening

Panic restricting my airways,

My throat all ablaze.

I rush to my bishop's home,

Tears streaking my cheeks wherever they want to roam.

Shame and guilt fill my very being,

Feel like fleeing.

Still, I gather my courage to share as commanded.

As he opens the door, his anger is so candid.

He demands to know why I couldn't make an appointment.

I feel like a fly in ointment.

As I tell him of my use of porn and masturbation,

His face grows even redder in all its anger and frustration.

He tells me he overcame it on his own and doesn't understand why I can't

And I must not really want it.

Shame and guilt ravage my soul,

His words stabbing like a sword as I bleed out my sins like ink on a scroll.

There they are for all to see, all to read.

All I can do is watch in horror as they witness my sexual greed.

He tells me I need to pray more fervently and study the scripture more.

They are the key and they are the door.

I pray and study multiple times a day,

But they don't stop my sexuality and I stumble as I walk away.

Back to my home, back to my hole.

There I will try again and again to pull myself out
of the lust of my burning inner coal.

Yet, it is all to no avail.

Against my own nature I will never prevail.

Years of my life are filled with bishops like this.

What is Adultery?

In those years of marriage, my wife's mind was filled with doubt and fear.

We often talked about my love for her and if it was clear.

You see, every time I masturbated, for her it was a betrayal.

As such, it weakened our bond and had her believe my love was frail.

I went out of my way to prove to her it was strong.

I gave up many freedoms to right what I had done wrong.

Each sexual act without my wife,

She viewed as adultery, a sin that took away our shared life.

In the end, she was right.

I was nothing but a blight.

I broke apart trying to be what she needed and the church demanded.

I just wasn't able to fit in even with all their actions, so heavy handed.

Welcome to the Club

Cycles of violence are difficult weapons to break,

Always circling their prey and leaving destruction
in their wake.

Sexual abuse is one such demonic tradition,

Clawing out wounds in the soul never to be seen by
a mortician.

Like a family heirloom, it's passed from generation
to generation,

Creating a people of no boundaries and yet a nation.

Welcome to the club, to the gang, to the tribe.

There's nothing to make it stop, nothing we can
prescribe.

The only way to halt this torture is to not pass it on,

To let the darkness seep out of you and to allow in
the dawn.

Chapter 2 – Misadventures

take two steps forward

healing isn't a straight line

now take one step back

Luck and Fuck

Misadventures are not chronological, but they do tend to happen less with time.

The hope is that you begin to move with life's rhythm and rhyme.

You learn and you grow.

Opportunities arise to demonstrate what you know.

With some faith and some luck,

You learn not to hurt others and yet not give too much of a fuck.

Partners Who Never Should Have Been

Some relationships never should have been.

I don't mean that they were a sin.

Rather I would say that they were better left alone,

Because all they were was destructive, a great
rolling stone.

One where you ran away,

One that left you with nothing to say.

For me, there were more of these than I'd like to
admit, but that didn't stop me,

I didn't learn or quit.

I kept on making the same mistakes again and
again,

My willful ignorance was my best friend.

One I remember in particular, was in high school,
you see.

A young lady who told me she had no boyfriend,
she was free.

When I kissed her though,

The next day her boyfriend walked up to me and
wanted to go.

I told him that I didn't want to fight,

But that didn't stop him from kicking my ass out of
spite.

After that the same girl refused to meet my gaze
from across the cafeteria or the hall,

She walked with the shame of a shadow knowing
she was partially to blame for the brawl.

I held onto my anger and let it grow over the next
year.

It soon took over and all my fear, it disappeared.

During a pickup basketball game, the same
boyfriend slandered and called me a name.

I saw red, a bright burning flame.

Next thing I knew, I had shoved him to the ground,

And went to work like some teenage version of
MMA pound and ground.

I only let up when he stopped moving,

And I woke up to realize there was nothing else I
was proving.

All these years later, I still have these horrors
floating around in my brain.

When they resurface it fills me with a mix of
misplaced pride and shame, and I question if I am
insane.

<u>Untold Love Confessions</u>

The secret tales of our hearts,

From there no wisp departs.

We speak them only in our minds,

A lockbox, perfect privacy it provides.

We gaze at the object of our obsession,

Knowing we'll never make confession.

Adoration from afar,

Burning desire like a shooting star.

No, we'll never share,

That hidden love for another goes nowhere.

First Kiss, Forbidden

That first kiss waiting, roses laid out on your jacket.

My words lost in some invisible bracket.

You walk towards me with sensual purpose.

I stand my ground, yet shaking deeply under the surface.

You lean in with one eyebrow cocked,

All my plans wash away, all sent to the ocean, all blocked.

Our lips connect and the fruit of that taste,

That forbidden first kiss I can never replace.

Sleeping Kiss

You drive over late at night,

After everyone turns off their light.

You walk up the steps and sit on the swing,

The very scent of you makes me want to scream.

We talk and laugh for hours on end,

Night slips towards day in our dreamland.

Finally, we lay down and hold each other tight,

Our lips touch for that sleeping kiss of the night.

Octopus Garden

The octopus garden can be quite a delight,

But it's not for everyone and that's alright.

We all have preferences best for us,

And figuring that out isn't any kind of fuss.

<u>Sacrilege</u>

There were times of thoughtless rebellion.

I was shaped like an angel with a streak of a hellion.

I didn't know or understand why I did what I did.

Looking back now, I realize it was because I hid.

I was hiding from all that fear and the shame.

All those titles of "addict" and "freak," giving me an ignoble fame.

It inundated me with tears and fears,

Not in a good way like with the band of so many audience cheers.

One such rebellion took the shape of an artist with a taste for the vampire bite.

Her fangs knew how to ignite me just right…

Pre-marital Whatever

I was taught to believe there is no sex before marriage.

To do such a thing is to disparage.

It denigrates what God has given only to a man and a woman.

To do such a thing is devilish and inhuman.

That meant that every time my fiancé and I ever touched each other on the fly…

I was the fall guy.

After all, I was the one with a "problem."

I was the monster, a faithless goblin.

When we met with her bishop to have the "sex talk,"

My questions left him with a face full of nothing but shock.

For example, I asked about oral sex.

He was disgusted and said a man never does or asks that from a woman he respects.

So…I was left emotionally alone and ashamed

As we entered this matrimonial bliss they proclaimed.

Enoch

A phone call with tears on the line,

All that's left are bloody sheets and brine,

That covers my lips with its salty taste,

All that potential life gone to waste.

Unlived life dead before it could begin,

My thoughts beat a deep and painful din.

So loud that my emotions and body are unclear,

There's nothing left but an overwhelming fear.

That loss, that was never supposed to have been,
wrapped like rope around my neck,

All that's left is that bloody splotch on the bed, a
speck.

I'm sorry you never were and will never get to be,

All I can give you is a name, the same one given to
me.

The Ghosts of Partners Past

There are so many ghosts of partners past that haunt my bed.

Their scents in my nose, their love nothing but dying memories in my head.

Each was a burning flame with a sweet incense.

Now they are empty words on my lips nothing but past tense.

I am grateful for the joys that we shared,

But mostly what remains are pain and wounds that can never be repaired.

Chapter 3 – Miracles

miracles abound

perceptions of such are rare

they are no less real

Passing Miracles

I have had many relationships end;

lovers, friends, even family.

They live on in my memories,

resurfacing like rogue waves

with the power to inundate my mind.

They steal in like thieves in the night

and stay as long as they wish.

I have but one choice…

and that is to invite them in

and wait them out.

And yet, there are others

that I need no reminding to invite into my heart and
soul.

They are memories of loved ones gone

for one reason or another

but who have left me more patient,

more courageous,

more empathetic,

and even wiser.

We might not be in one another's lives anymore,

but my life is richer for them…

that in and of itself is a miracle.

Butterfly Kisses

Years later I can still remember that night,

A bunch of us at your house hanging out. It was a
warm summer evening, the sky so bright.

We were playing games and laughing and just
having fun.

You and I gravitated towards each other. As we
chatted more, I could feel those butterflies and I
thought I might run.

But you kept me there with those eyes and that
smile.

I couldn't drink it up fast enough. I fell into your
eyes like my own personal tropical isle.

Then that smile on your face subtly shifted.

I could feel it in my blood. Some invisible barrier
between us lifted.

You asked me if I knew about the butterfly kiss.

I didn't respond, knowing they all flew in my stomach. You leaned in and brushed your eyelash on my cheek…and I entered a state of bliss.

That evening was the only time we ever really shared.

Our lives moved in different directions. That moment of healthy intimacy though just can't be compared.

Still Friends

Thank you so much for being willing to still be my friend,

For continuing to share your life with me even after our love's end.

<u>Seeing is Believing</u>

Hello beautiful stranger, it's so nice to meet you.

Thank you so much for *seeing* me.

It's a miracle that you *see* something that I didn't even know was there.

It's wonder and awe I *see* in your eyes and I can't explain it.

How can that be when you are smiling at ME?

Where did this sunshine and light come from that you are bathing in?

There's goodness in me?

I had no idea.

Thank you so much for showing me.

Tears for Me

Your tears are for me.

Your wound opened when I left.

You said that you would be okay and I know now that you are.

You moved on with your life,

But that night you cried for me.

For me.

I am grateful that I meant enough to you that you shed tears for me.

For me.

Open Doors

Thank you so much for never giving up on me.

You are the partner who continues to be a part of my life to some degree.

You have continued to support my life.

We worked so hard to overcome our bitterness and strife.

Although we may not be partners, lovers, or even friends anymore.

I'm grateful we always have for each other an open door.

More Than Trauma

Thank you to that long ago partner who let me know I was more than my trauma,

Who held me in the middle of the night in my ugly pajama.

Love Multiplies

I will always remember all the lessons you gave.

You helped me embrace my truth, my orientation, my name.

You will forever have my thanks for this fresh reality.

The new sacred place where I hold dearly every attribute, each nook of my personality.

I will always remember that love does not divide.

Love multiplies and that is something that I will not hide.

<u>Not the Sum of My Mistakes</u>

Thank you to that long ago partner who let me know again and again,

That I was not the sum of my mistakes, that they were not the end.

Hiding in Plain Sight

There you were hiding in plain sight,

I have to admit that when I realized what had
happened, it gave me a little bit of a fright.

We had worked together for over a year,

And I thought our friendship was destined to be
platonic, but clearly I am no seer.

When I finally realized how I felt,

You were pulling weeds and I came over and knelt,

Besides you to ask if we could go out.

Your face so full of expression shouted its wonder
at what I was about.

I explained myself and what I was feeling.

You still looked like you had bumped your head on
a high ceiling.

Still, you said you would like to try it out.

We both realized quickly after that there was no doubt.

Now it's been years since that moment in the grass,

And I'm still so grateful you said yes instead of kicking my ass.

Chapter 4 – Mythologies

sex is not a shame

it is bonding and a game

there's no need for blame

Incubus Games

We walk upstairs and I lay her down,

She wears her bare body like a glimmering crown.

Leather straps tie her to the bed,

I stare at her with a hunger that needs to be fed.

I move slowly, worshipping her body,

Everything I do is sensually naughty.

At first she moans, then pleads, then begs,

But I don't stop till she has shaking legs.

These are those moments of midnight flames,

These are my insatiable incubus games.

Old Flames

I lust for those old flames at times,

Even though I know they burn.

Their glowing lights still call me,

That warm flame for which I yearn.

I learn though what I need to do,

What I need to resist.

I remind myself of the anger of that flame,

How it is only rage from which it can subsist.

Flower's Nectar

Who knew that a flower could taste so sweet?

That nether nectar dripping like a candy treat.

I can't believe it tastes so good.

I nudge my face in under the hood.

I lick it up greedily.

I'm so excited I don't care about my own indecency.

I play with it in my mouth.

The only thing I regret is not moving sooner to the South.

Graveyard

Golden hair framed by blue skies,

As I look up into your green eyes.

A moment of purest connection,

Erotic and spiritual, a human collection

Of some of the sweetest moments we can share,

Bound in flesh, among graves, our orgasmic prayer,

To Divinity both above and below,

Who imbue us with a sensual glow.

Our love making is a celebration of the life the dead
also once held

A ritual of living, as our bodies together we do
weave and meld.

Cowgirls

I am a big believer in the statement that dreams DO come true.

Our threesome was like wild animals in a zoo.

She was riding my cock and you sat on my face.

We all came together, blasting off into outer space.

Samhain Succubus

She stands before me, this succubus queen.

Alabaster skin and eyes a piercing green.

Curled ram's horns and leathery bat wings.

A flowing black dress and a body that sings.

She stares at me and crooks her finger.

I hasten over, I know not to linger.

She caresses my face and places her hands in my hair.

Then she pushes me down so I can serve her with a sensual prayer.

My devotion lasts far into the night.

I worship this succubus queen in our sexual rite.

Circe

Whitest sash and flowing gown of marble,
The sorceress erect, my thoughts garble.

She sashays solicitous towards me,
I fall to my knees in a voiceless plea.

Her eyebrow cocks hard and her eyes glow green,
A smirk smears her face, sensually obscene.

She slides softly her gown over my head,
Laying bare her thighs, a delicious spread.

At their center that sweetest honey pot,
Beckons me to claim it my private lot.

I lean forward to nuzzle that bare mound,
My intention, in her nectar to drown.

I take my first taste of that divine sap,
Searching each crevice of that female map.

My drinking is slow and steady at first,
But soon I can't stop my deepening thirst.

I delve deeper and longer with my strokes,
Yearning to bring that ecstasy, to coax

All that delightful juice forth to my lips,
And then she releases, bucking her hips.

I cling to her as if a nursing babe,
Longing to insist that instance we save

As an eternity in a moment,
That we might drive all our lust to foment.

My wish is granted as she grabs my face,
She pulls me to my feet in heated chase.

Enoch Black

That hunger gleams intensely in her eyes,
I know without words what will be her prize.

Now to her knees she shifts so eagerly,
Speechless and still I stand there meagerly.

Her hands caress me gently through my pants,
The rhythm like some silent, erotic chants.

She grins at my bulging need to be free,
Her eyes are glazed with such lustful glee.

She can tell that I am about to burst,
She licks her lips at me showing *her* thirst.

She unzips my pants oh so very slow.
Her tongue and mouth always know where to go.

She sucks me fast and so hard to the edge.
Her body holds my orgasm as a pledge.

She slowly slides my cock out of her mouth.

She stands once more, our journey shall move
south.

She strips my clothes and lays me on the bed.

She ties my hands and gives me more deep head.

Finally though the moment has arrived.

She mounts me, no more will I be deprived.

Her rhythm is slow and so slippery smooth.

My aching cock she is going to soothe.

Faster and harder, she picks up the pace.

Together we're about to win this race.

I buck hard into her hips as we crash.

It's only us, the world's gone in a flash.

Library Lasciviousness

Long black skirt and red blouse with a pencil in her
hair,

Walking with clicking heals as many heads turn
quietly to stare.

She heads upstairs to the family bathroom and click
goes the lock,

She waits patiently until she hears a faint knock.

She unlocks the door and I slip right in,

Staring at that façade of a librarian, eyes full of sin.

She leans against the bathroom wall,

And motions for me to crawl.

I inch my way over to the corner,

Staring up just to adore her.

My hands slide up her thighs and realize it's bare
under there,

I growl in hunger like a grizzly bear.

I won't wait any longer, I nibble my way up till I get to her mound,

My tongue is slow and luxurious at first, but then I begin to pound.

I flick faster and faster while her hands pull at my hair,

Finally, she cums hard in my mouth, her juices in my beard and everywhere.

Clawing lightly at her body as she calms down,

I wear her nectar like a liquid crown.

She pulls me gently to my feet,

Then kneels and looks up at me oh so sweet.

Her hands caress my pants enlarging all my lust,

My bulge gets so hard all I want to do is thrust,

But she continues to tease me with her hands,

till finally she unzips my pants showing me she understands

That I need her mouth caressing me soft and deep,

And she takes me in smoothly, not making a peep.

Her rhythm is slow and long at first,

Then increases in speed with her thirst.

I know I won't last much longer,

But she doesn't mind and sucks even stronger.

Down her throat I pour my milk,

Her hair in my hands is just like silk.

A satisfied cat's smile quirks her lip,

As she continues to play with my tip.

We smile wickedly at each other as we walk out,

In the library there's no scream, no shout.

No one's there to tell us what bad little children we've been,

No one knows of our secret library sin.

Count Down

Hey baby, want to play a game?

You do as I say,

That's how we'll play.

That's right, nod your head,

You understood what I said.

Now take off your clothes and feel the air on your skin.

Get ready because we are both about to sin.

See how your nipples get hard.

Pull on them, all your inhibitions you can disregard.

That's good, you can feel the heat now. Turn yourself on with your hands.

Obey all of my commands.

Slide them down your hips and thighs.

Stare at me with those heavy-lidded eyes.

Good, now slowly peel back those lips.

Let your fingers inside that wet eclipse.

Yes, that's it, you can feel that heat rise.

Do as I say and you'll win your prize.

Work that clit nice and slow.

Steady now as we go.

Ready darling for the last part? Perfect.

This is how we'll start.

I'm going to count down from ten.

And then you will cum like I said.

Ten…go real slow. Listen to me.

Nine. Soon you will be free.

Eight. Rub a bit faster my dear.

Should I whisper the numbers in your ear?

Seven. We're getting so close.

Six. Soon you'll have an orgasmic dose.

Five. I see that juice on your fingers.

Four. Fast now. Don't hold back. We can't linger.

Three. Don't hold your breath, we're almost there.

Two. Beg me to cum. Say it like a prayer.

One...hold it please. I want you to have one last tease.

Zero...that's it, baby. Now cum for me!

Mmmmm. You're such a good girl. You did so well.

I love having you under my commanding spell.

Green Light, Red Light

Go ahead and lay down on the bed,

Now take your clothes off and your pussy will be fed.

Turn the vibrator on low,

Run it in circles on your clit really slow.

Know that I'm getting hard just watching you,

I'm going to help you cum, it's true.

First though we're going to play a little game.

It will help build up your burning orgasmic flame.

I will tell you this right now, my sweet.

It will be a sexy little treat.

Here's what I want you to do.

When I tell you to stop, you're going to do it, my boo.

Keep going and turn it up to medium and let it get a
bit lit,

Nice long, slow circles around your sweet clit.

Red Light…now you stop like the good girl that
you are.

Don't make me punish you from afar.

That's right, no touching between us just yet.

You need to obey and you need to sweat.

I want to know that you can and will stop.

That's it, my sub, now get ready to pop.

Turn that vibrator all the way to high.

You're about to cum so hard you'll cry.

Red Light! Don't you dare burst yet.

Good girl, my sweet little pet.

Your obedience makes me so hard, it's time for us both.

Green light and let's fulfill our mutual, sexual oath.

Mmmmm.

<u>Chapter 5 – Mindfulness</u>

present here and now

breathing in each other's scent

mindfully loving

Unfulfilling Love

Have you ever had that secret thought inside?

There's that special someone you need to love just to feel alive.

Yet, it doesn't work when you're together,

The best thing you can do is to cut the tether.

Still, it leaves you with a hole in your heart,

No matter though, because you are happier apart.

You learn to live with the pain,

Because being together was like being insane.

Be grateful for the courage you had to leave,

You have so many new stories and adventures to weave.

Share Your Joys and Passions

Please don't just share a bed with your lover.

Share your life with them, show them there's so much to discover.

When you get home from work,

Give them a hug and a teasing smirk.

Listen to the ups and downs of their day.

Light their path when they can't find their way.

Share all your passions and joy.

Laugh much, be silly, and even coy.

These small matters a great difference will make

As you face all that daily pain and ache.

<u>Beginner's Mind</u>

Let this be the first time you join.

Allow it to be the other side of the same coin.

Breathe in a new beginning of love.

Breathe out beliefs that it's the same old glove.

Realize that each time is unique.

Let the rush of newness blossom on your cheek.

May beginner's mind lead you down the same road

That you may know it's different every time, this
lover's ode.

Being Present

Be present as your lover nibbles your ear with a fervor you won't soon forget.

Let them caress your face in a manner neither of you will ever regret.

Be present as their head between your legs casts a lustful silhouette.

Let your lovemaking be a harmonious duet.

Be present as they make you burn with desire and sweat.

Fill your bed with thunderous orgasms like rolling waves so wet.

Setting the Scene

Set the mood just right.

Light the candles and brighten the night.

Lay your body next to theirs.

Show them the you who always cares.

Fill up on their scent.

Let not your love be spent.

No, hold them warm in your bed.

Let your bodies share all that would be said.

Breathing

Breathe in their scent.

May it your love augment.

Breathe out your joy.

May it their trust employ.

Breathe in their hope.

May it increase your perspective on love, your scope.

Breathe out your faith.

May it stave off their doubtful wraith.

Breathe in their being.

May it be for your freeing.

Breathe out your soul.

May it them always console.

Staring into Each Other's Eyes

Gaze into their eyes, the windows of the soul.

Let their heart bloom for you, opening like a sacred scroll.

Percolate on the various colors of their iris.

Each one is symbolic of what you find desirous.

Hues of gold,

All their stories still unshared and untold.

Pools of emerald green,

Their mysteries yet unseen.

Dallops of molten brown,

Images of their love for you like an oaken crown.

Slithers of sky blue,

Their adoration for you showing through.

Drink up their internal light.

May it guide you to a love most kind and bright.

Sensual Massage

Wash your partner in the shower, head to toe.

Go sensual and slow.

Let them know you want to memorize their body.

Demonstrate to them that what comes next will be even more naughty.

Take them to the bed.

Lay them down in silk so red.

Apply oil to their shoulders and back.

Whisper to them about how they're your favorite snack.

Turn them over and rub some more.

Give them all you have, till they can burn to their core.

Spooning

The most magical of sleeping potions,
Body heat and scents better than lotions.

An elixir of nudity and sheets,
Carved into one form of sensual treats.

Breathing in and creating one being,
Immersed in each other, oh so freeing.

To have and to hold one in such a way,
Leaving behind time, satisfied to stay.

Here in this moment of physical bliss,
Spooning is a paramour's dreaming kiss.

Hug

Hug your lover longer than is needed.

It's how the garden of love is seeded.

Acknowledgments

First and foremost, I want to thank you, dear reader, for taking a chance on my writing and me. Thank you for allowing me to share a small but extremely vulnerable aspect of myself with you. I am so grateful for the opportunity.

To the Instagram poetry communities, I write a big thank you. So many of you have been supportive of my poetic endeavors and patient with my grotesque love of dragons. Thank you for putting up with me.

This collection would not have been nearly as beautiful and so well put-together if not for the efforts and kindness of Ravven White at Curious Corvid Publishing. Ravven and I have shared many a poetic adventure and I look forward to more. Thank you, my dear PIP, my Partner in Poetry, for all of your support and unrelenting, disgusting optimism.

To my furry feline friend and companion, Rowan…thank you for keeping me seated at home so many hours with your warm body…basically forcing me to write…and train my bladder in a way only cats sleeping on your lap can do.

Finally, to my "home," my loved ones here with me physically and emotionally. You know who you are. Your love, support, and patience with my madness, however much method to it there might be, grant me some semblance of sanity, allowing me the ability to the see the beauty in darkness and to embrace the light as part of myself.

You can read more of Enoch's poetry and stay up to date with his projects on Instagram @stormdragonlibrary.